Party Planning Tips

for

The Clueless Chick™

Sourced Media Books, LLC
20 Via Cristobal
San Clemente, CA 92673
www.sourcedmediabooks.com

ISBN-13: 978-1-937458-07-2

LCCN: 2012910464

Printed in the United States of America.

This publication is designed to provide entertainment value and is sold with the understanding that the publisher is not engaged in rendering legal, accounting, or other professional advice of any kind. If legal advice or other expert assistance is required, the services of a competent professional person should be sought.

—From a Declaration of Principles jointly adopted by a Committee of the American Bar Association and a Committee of Publishers and Associations

Party Planning Tips
for
The Clueless Chick™

Jennifer Durbin

Sourced Media Books, LLC
San Clemente, CA

To Colleen, for pushing me to be everything you knew I could be.

Contents

Foreword

*P*arty Planning Tips for The Clueless Chick™ is the third in a series of pocket guides for the professional woman, who would spend hours upon hours planning and reviewing websites if she had more than five minutes to spare in her busy day. Written by the quintessential Type-A/OCD overachiever, *The Clueless Chick™* is a collection of pocket guides for navigating through the milestones and obstacles all women, girlfriends, wives, and mothers face. First and foremost, I do not claim to be an expert party planner, although I do plan parties professionally in my spare time. What I am is a woman just like you, albeit a little obsessed with over-researching life's little challenges, and I'd like to share what I've learned from my experiences (and mistakes). My hope is that I will be able to save you hours of research and days of searching hundreds of websites in your quest for the one kernel of knowledge you are looking for. *Party Planning Tips for The Clueless Chick™* will afford you the time to focus on the fun parts of party planning and help you avoid some of the common pitfalls of poor planning. When you are finished with this pocket guide, you will feel less "clueless"—armed with a roadmap to follow through party planning.

Party Planning Tips for The Clueless Chick™ is a compilation of everything I wish I had known before I planned my first party. You can think of this as a party planning quick-start guide based on all of the research I have done over the years. My party planning advice comes straight from my experiences, the experiences of my friends, and the countless magazines, websites, and TV shows I have studied in my neverending efforts to plan the perfect party. I have been planning parties and making favors for friends and family for as long as I can remember. In 2009, after throwing an epic cooking shower for a dear friend, I lost count of the number of times guests and the professional chef performing the cooking demonstration asked, "Jennifer, why are you not doing this professionally?!" Within a month, my small business, The Clueless Chick™, was born. The following month, The Clueless Chick™ had designed its first bridal shower.

Whether you are about to plan your first party or you are simply looking for tips to make party planning easier, this is the book for you! I'll walk you through all of the major steps of party planning, from setting a budget to determining whether you need to hire a professional party planner to cleaning up after the big event. I will share with you a number of sample parties to inspire your creative bone or to get the ball rolling. I'll provide you with tips you can refer back to every time you have a new party to plan. With a little help from The Clueless Chick™, you'll be planning parties like a pro (or know when to hire a pro instead of trying to do it all yourself). I am here to clue you in!

There are two terms I use throughout this book that deserve a bit of clarification. To avoid the unsightly "Host/Hostess" and "He/She" throughout the book, I generically refer to the individual hosting the party as "Hostess" and the guest of honor as "She." Now let's get planning!

1

Party Planning

Congratulations! You have something to celebrate, and someone special is counting on you to throw a great party. Party planning doesn't have to be hard, expensive, or time-consuming; with the right prep work, party planning can be fun and stress-free. Every party is as unique as its hostess, but you will find that the core planning process is the same for a Sunday dinner for six or a 50th anniversary party for two hundred.

The key to planning a good party is to stay organized. There is almost nothing more frustrating than addressing your invitations, only to realize that you have fifty five people on your guest list and only fifty invitations. How do you avoid a mishap like that? Keep good notes! The easiest way to do this is by following The Clueless Chick's Party Planning Checklist:

Party Planning Checklist
for The Clueless Chick™

- ☐ Event   _____
- ☐ Date   _____
- ☐ Time   _____
- ☐ Guest Count   _____
- ☐ Budget   _____
- ☐ Theme   _____
- ☐ Invitations   _____
- ☐ Decorations   _____
- ☐ Favors   _____
- ☐ Entertainment   _____
- ☐ Menu   _____

    Food   _____

    Drinks   _____

- ☐ Timeline   _____

              _____

- ☐   _____
- ☐   _____

Don't worry if you don't yet know where to start. In just a few chapters, you will know exactly how to fill in the blanks with ease.

Top Considerations During Preplanning

☐ Date: Pick a date and time convenient for you and your guest of honor. Don't let a major event spoil your party— check local events, calendars, and sports schedules before you lock in a date and time. Or get creative and make your party the "pre-game" or "after" party. There is almost nothing worse than sending out invitations, only to find that half of your guests are going to a concert that day.

☐ Guest list: Estimate the guest count so that you can appropriately plan.

☐ Budget.

☐ Party planner: Will you hire a professional party planner? Party planners are great resources who can help you with every last detail, or just the big ones.

Budget

Once you have decided to plan a party, one of the first decisions you will need to make is how much money you are comfortable spending on your event. By setting your budget early, you can save yourself time and avoid some stress. For example, if you know that you are able to afford spending two dollars per favor and you focus your search accordingly, you will avoid the disappointment of falling in love with ten-dollar favors. If you are fortunate enough to have a limitless budget for your party, let's be honest, you're not reading my book. For the rest of you Chicks, let's set a budget!

Party Budget
for The Clueless Chick™

☐ Location and Coordination   _____

    Location rental fee   _____

    Rentals (tables, chairs,
    linens, etc.)   _____

    Party planner   _____

☐ Invitations   _____

    Invitations/adornments   _____

    Postage   _____

☐ Decorations   _____

☐ Favors   _____

☐ Entertainment   _____

    Music   _____

    Games   _____

☐ Menu   _____

    Food   _____

    Drinks   _____

☐ Paper Products   _____

    Tableware (plates, napkins,
    flatware)   _____

    Glassware   _____

☐ Labor (setup/cleanup,
food service, babysitter, etc.)   _____

☐   _____

☐   _____

    Total $ _____

Like any budget, you can approach your party budget from the top down or the bottom up. If you know you have one hundred dollars to spend on your event, simply back in to each individual line item. It is also important to prioritize each line item, should you need to adjust your budget. If food is the most important aspect of the party, you may need to cut your decorations budget if food ends up costing more than you originally anticipated.

When you begin to shop for everything included in your budget, you may find that prices are higher or lower than you anticipated—so be prepared to be flexible.

Once you have an idea of the type of party you want to have and how much you plan to spend, the next step is to decide if you are going to do all of the work yourself, or if you will hire a professional party planner to do some or all of the work for you. If you decide to plan the party on your own, you've come to the right place! You have a lot of work ahead of you, but I will make it as stress-free as possible.

Hiring a Party Planner

If the thought of planning a party has you in a cold sweat, you may want to consider hiring a professional party planner. You will find that a party planner is a must in certain situations if you are totally out of your league or simply do not have the time to devote to planning the party. Party planners can save you a good bit of time and have resources available that you might otherwise not have access to. For instance, they will know off the top of their head which locations are perfect for your event or the best caterer for you. A good party planner can make planning a stress-free process and allow you to simply enjoy your party! Most party planners offer a variety of service levels that range from helping you choose a theme (à la carte) to planning your entire event (full-service). The level of service you choose will depend on your needs as well as your budget. A party planner may charge a flat fee, an hourly rate, or a percentage of the total event budget. It is very important to have your budget set before you begin looking for a party planner to ensure that you choose the right services for your budget.

Finding the right party planner for your event is just like finding the right photographer—the right party planner will capture the essence of you in the event, while the wrong party planner will leave you with a party you would have rather not hosted (or worse, attended). The good news is that it is not hard to find the right party planner for you! Party planning has become a very popular career, so it should not be hard to find a few party planners in your area. Whether you choose a professional party planner who has been entertaining for twenty years, or a recent graduate who is just starting her business, it is important to find one with whom you enjoy working.

How to Find a Party Planner?

- ☐ International Special Events Society (Certified Special Events Professionals); see www.ises.com.

- ☐ The Knot (www.theknot.com). After all, a wedding is the ultimate party!

- ☐ Ask a friend who recently threw a fabulous event whom she hired.

- ☐ Check your local Small Business Association.

- ☐ Call the venue you would like to use and ask if there are party planners they recommend using. You may also discover that the location provides a party planner as part of the package.

☐ Google "party planner" and your city.

Questions to Ask a Party Planner

☐ Qualifications

- How long have you been planning events?
- Are you a Certified Special Events Professional (CSEP)?
- Have you planned events like mine before?
- Are you affiliated with any of the local or national event planning associations?

☐ Fees

- What are your fees?
- What forms of payment do you accept?
- Can I revise the level of service I am purchasing?
- Do you require that I sign a contract to retain your services?

☐ Style

- How will you communicate with me throughout the planning process?
- Will you be available to answer general party questions? Via phone? Via email?

☐ Other

- Can you work within my party budget?
- Do you have an assistant/backup in case you are ill or unable to attend my event?
- Are there local vendors you have worked with before that you can recommend to me?
- Have you planned events at the location I am considering?

Once you have found the perfect party planner for you, it is time to get down to business! When you meet your party planner to start planning your party, be prepared to share your ideas. The more information you share with her, the better your event will be. Party planners are great, but they aren't mind readers. That being said, don't be surprised if she comes up with exactly the idea you have been trying to put into words. Most importantly, be prepared to share your party budget so that your party planner can plan appropriately. It is very disappointing to hear all of her fabulous ideas, only to learn that they will cost $5,000 when your budget is $1,000.

How to Use This Book if You Hire a Party Planner

- Focus on the chapters that talk about the items you will be managing (guest list, being a good hostess, etc.).
- Use the checklists to track everything the party planner is doing for you.
- Use "Get Inspired!" to get inspired. ☺

Get Inspired!

Planning a party can feel like a daunting task, but it doesn't have to be! There are countless ways to get inspired or excited about party planning. When you're drawing a blank about what to do for your best friend's baby shower or your boyfriend's surprise 30th birthday party, just do a little searching and you're sure to find inspiration. It's important to open yourself up to be inspired by unlikely sources. I've been inspired by a window display, a T-shirt, or whatever happens to be on sale at the party store or Target. I've even planned an entire party theme around cute plates I found on sale at a department store.

How The Clueless Chick™ Takes Inspiration to the Next Level

- **Great find/inspiration:** Square salad plates with blue and green fork and knife outlines painted on the side
- **Theme:** Cooking bridal shower
- **Invitations:** A cute kitchen scene background with an enclosed recipe card and a note asking guests to put their favorite recipe on the card for the bride's collection
- **Decorations:** Cooking utensil bouquets, kitchen towel cake, personalized aprons for the bride, mother of the bride, and mother of the groom
- **Favors:** Personalized boxes filled with an apron, recipe cards, pan scraper, and or heart shaped measuring spoons
- **Entertainment:** Cooking demonstration by a local chef

You can also find great inspiration from the experts. Don't be overwhelmed by how perfect their parties are; you don't have to be Martha Stewart to throw a fantastic party (that just makes it a lot easier). The goal is always to have the best party possible for your guest of honor within your budget. Here are a few of my favorite party planning resources.

- ☐ Websites
  - www.marthastewart.com
  - www.celebrations.com
  - www.foodnetwork.com
  - www.party411.com
  - www.thepartydress.net
  - www.CluelessChick.com (shameless plug)
- ☐ Party blogs
  - www.hostessblog.com
  - www.partyplanningmom.blogspot.com

☐ Magazines
- *Martha Stewart Living*
- *Southern Living*
- *Every Day with Rachel Ray*
- *Real Simple*

Fun Ways to Find Inspiration on Your Own

☐ Go shopping.
- Spend a little time walking around your local party, stationery, or craft store, or do a little online shopping. Many stores will also have free craft idea cards for inspiration. You may also have luck walking through the party aisle at Target or Wal-Mart.

☐ Think about your guest of honor or your guests at large.
- What is your guest of honor's favorite sport, game, candy, toy, movie, band, color, etc.?
- Do you have any guests who are vegan? If so, you may want to steer clear of an ice cream party.

Planning Your Party Style

Now that you have some ideas under your belt, it's time to get down to business! It's important to focus on your party style early in the planning process, because your style will carry through your theme, invitations, and decorations. Don't worry, you don't have to be super creative or even super specific about your party style to throw a successful party. You may simply decide that for the adoption shower you are planning, your style will be modern elegance with your core colors being green and silver. Now let's get planning!

Theme

Before you work out the nitty-gritty details of your party, like what invitations you will send and what food you will serve, you first need to decide on your theme. Keeping your party style in mind, you will want to choose a theme that is not only appropriate for your event, but also fun and unique. Having a theme does not always mean spending a lot of money! If you shop smart and plan ahead, nearly any theme is possible at any time during the year. Your imagination and your budget are your only limits.

Choosing red as your core party color in late February can save you a lot of money. Simply shop all of the after Valentines Day sales on February 15th and pick up everything you need at fifty percent off!

When you are picking your theme, keep in mind that you will want your invitations, decorations, entertainment, and menu to complement your theme. This is, of course, easiest when you choose either a flexible or trendy theme such as specific colors or the current top cartoon. It also makes planning a good bit easier if you use the current season as inspiration; you're much more likely to find supplies for your football party during football season. You may also choose to use last season as inspiration if you are able to find everything you need on sale.

You can make a party, especially a shower or birthday party, extra special by choosing a personal theme. For instance, choose a theme that relates to the guest of honor's favorite sports team or favorite color. There is almost nothing better than having your guest of honor walk into the party and say, "Oh! That's my favorite ____!"

Easy Ways to Pick a Party Theme

- ☐ Find a cute invitation.
- ☐ Use the season as inspiration.
- ☐ Build a theme around the gift you have purchased for the guest of honor.
- ☐ Find a great deal on party supplies and work around the style.
- ☐ Google! Just search for the guest of honor's favorite things + "party" on Google Images and see what you get (i.e., "pedicure party").

Things to Keep in Mind When Choosing a Theme

- ☐ The time of year
  - It can be tricky to throw a Valentine's theme party in October.
- ☐ Your guest list
  - Are you inviting enough guests, or too many, to pull off your theme? Do any of your guests have severe allergies? A PB&J theme party is not a good idea if a number of your guests are allergic to peanuts!
- ☐ Budget
  - Can you afford to pull off your theme?
- ☐ Date and time
  - Is the time of your party appropriate for your theme? A cocktail party is a little tricky over Sunday brunch.
- ☐ Guest of honor

- Does your theme fit his/her style and personality? A camping shower might not be a good idea for a girl who wouldn't be caught dead without her Manolo Blahniks.

Location

Picking a location for your party may have been part of your theme decision, or it may have been a foregone conclusion that your housewarming party will be at your house. Personally, I prefer to have parties at home—everyone is more comfortable, your options are nearly limitless, you have plenty of time to set up and clean up, and you are in complete control (ideal for a control freak like me!). Entertaining at home is also a lot cheaper than renting a space. However, if you do not have sufficient space in your home to comfortably fit all of your guests, you'll need to find another location or consider having the party during a season where you can utilize your deck or yard. You will also need to take into consideration whether your home is appropriate for your party and if you have the time and energy to clean up both before and after the party. The good news is that there are plenty of location options for every budget.

Types of Locations

All-Inclusive (restaurants, country clubs, etc.)

- ☐ Pros
  - They do much of the work for you—setup, decorating, cleanup, etc.
  - They often provide all food and drinks
  - They may provide an event coordinator for you
  - Some locations may even provide favors for guests
  - Basically, they do all of the heavy lifting for you!

☐ Cons

- There may be restrictions on the decorations you can use.

- You may not be allowed to bring in any outside food such as a cake from your favorite bakery.

- It can be hard to cut corners when everything is included.

- You may need to book the location well in advance, or schedule the party during a non-peak time (a non-refundable deposit is usually required).

- You may have limited access to the location before and after your designated time.

Activity-Based (Paint your own pottery studio, batting cages, museum, bouncy house gym, etc.)

☐ Pros

- They may do much of the work for you — setup, decorating, cleanup, etc.

- You do not need to worry about planning an activity, or even your party's timeline.

- Some locations may even give you preprinted invitations to send.

- Everyone is virtually guaranteed to be entertained.

☐ Cons

- Some do not allow you to serve food or drinks, specifically alcohol.

- Some require a minimum purchase or a room rental fee.

- Your party may feel just like the party you attended at the same location last year.

- You may need to book the location well in advance of the party or schedule the party during an off-peak time (a non-refundable deposit may be required).
- You may have limited access to the location before and after your designated time.

Open Space (Conference center, ballroom, etc.)

☐ Pros

- With the right decorations, you can transform the space into just about anything.
- This is a relatively inexpensive way to rent a very large space equipped to handle most anything you need to set up.
- The facility will likely have a list of approved/ recommended vendors.
- The facility may provide staff to clean up the space after your party.

☐ Cons

- You may need to do a good bit of decorating and secure tables, seating, etc.
- You still have to coordinate food, drinks, entertainment, etc.
- There may be a limited list of vendors you are allowed to use.
- You may have limited access to the location before and after your designated time.

Free Locations (park, public pool, etc.)

☐ Pros

- It's free!

- You have the flexibility to design whatever type of event you choose.
- There are often built-in activity areas, such as pools or playgrounds.

☐ Cons
- Use of the space may be on a first-come, first-served basis, which can be risky.
- If the location is outside, you may only be able to use it during daylight hours, and if it rains, you're going to get wet! ☺
- You are responsible for all setup, cleanup, and everything in between.
- If the location is in a public area, it may be hard to control who is milling around.

Finding the Right Location

Now that you know what the pros and cons are for each type of location, it is time to determine what your local options are. Once you have narrowed down your list of potential locations, it is a good idea to visit two to three of them for comparison. Great local location resources include:

☐ Your city's Convention and Visitors Bureau.

☐ City Search (www.citysearch.com)

☐ Local restaurant, hotel, and event space listings.

☐ Ask one of the vendors you have already selected if she would recommend any local spots.

☐ Search local blogs.

☐ Ask a friend or neighbor for recommendations.

Questions to Ask a Location Representative

☐ Is your location available on _____?

☐ How many people can you comfortably accommodate?

☐ Do you offer any event packages?

☐ Do you provide an event coordinator?

☐ What are your fees?

☐ Do you require a deposit to book your location?

☐ What forms of payment do you accept?

☐ Am I allowed to bring my own food or drinks?

☐ Do you have a list of recommended/approved vendors?

☐ Do you allow alcohol to be served?

☐ Do you provide tables, chairs, and linens?

☐ Do you provide assistance to set up and clean up?

☐ Can I access your location before the event to set up?

☐ Do you have any restrictions on the use of your space (decorations, games, etc.)?

☐ Are there any other policies I need to be aware of?

Invitations

Your invitation is the first glimpse your guests have into your event (the style, formality, etc.)—and the only part of your party that guests who are unable to attend will see. Make them count by taking time to choose the right wording, and address them with care. There are nearly endless invitation options, countless retailers, and multiple format options. If you are going the more traditional/formal route and ordering paper invitations, you'll want to visit your local stationery store, search online, or consider making your own. If you want to go the paperless route, you may have just as much work to do, since these days you have a number of options.

Traditional Invitation Tips

☐ Order/make matching thank-you notes (either for yourself or as a gift for the guest of honor).

☐ Include any special parking instructions or directions.

☐ Get a few extra invitations and envelopes, just in case.

☐ Use cute stickers that coordinate with your theme as envelope closures—who wants to lick a bunch of envelopes?

Your Local Stationery Store

Support your local economy by shopping at your local stationery store, be it a national chain or a locally owned business! Not only is this the best way to receive one-on-one expert advice, but you will also have the chance to learn about the latest trends and unique options. Unlike searching through a million invitations online, in a stationery store you are actually able to feel the sample's weight, quality, etc. But be prepared to lose track of time flipping through all of their amazing sample books. If you are feeling overwhelmed by all of your options, it helps to clearly explain your vision to the stationer so that she will show you only the sample books that fit your party's style (yet another reason why picking your party style and theme comes before invitations).

Shop Online

If you don't find exactly what you are looking for at your local stationery store, or if you are more comfortable surfing the Web, you are in luck because there are many options. The nice thing about many of the online retailers is the ability to filter the invitations by price, size, color, theme, etc. But be careful—you can lose hours and hours searching online. You will need to pay close attention to the item details to ensure that the paper weight is exactly what you are looking for.

As with any purchase, you need to be careful to choose a reputable retailer. If there happens to be an error with your order, it can be difficult and very time-consuming to make an exchange.

Here are a few of my favorite online invitation retailers:

- ☐ www.tinyprints.com
- ☐ www.peartreegreetings.com
- ☐ www.tickledpinkdesign.net
- ☐ www.invitationbox.com
- ☐ www.invitationconsultants.com
- ☐ www.shutterfly.com
- ☐ www.polkadotdesign.com
- ☐ www.minted.com

DIY Options

For those of you Chicks who want to get a little crafty or are looking for a way to save some money but still send out traditional invitations, it is time to discover your inner DIYer! Whether you are an avid stamper or crafter, or you have never before done anything crafty, you can fairly easily make your own invitations.

DIY invitations can vary from the preprinted, fill-in-the-blank invitations you find at the party store to custom stamped, embossed, and embellished invitations. I find that it is easiest and most cost-effective to create an invitation somewhere in between.

Tips for Making Your Own Invitations

☐ Purchase cardstock and 5 x 7" envelopes at your local office supply store and print two invitations per page on your home printer. Then simply cut and stuff! If you are feeling extra crafty, add an additional layer of colored cardstock or embellishments.

☐ Skip the envelopes and print double-sided postcards on your home printer.

☐ Purchase designer stationery and envelopes at your local stationery or office supply store and print on your home printer. Be careful to take any pre-printed designs into account before designing your invitations.

☐ If you have elegant handwriting or a friend who owes you a favor (and has time), handwrite the invitations.

Tips for Designing Your Own Invitations

☐ Download free clipart online, use a picture of the guest of honor, or get crafty with word art.

☐ Create your invitation in Word/Pages (or any word processing program); reset your margins or work within an appropriately sized text box.

☐ To ensure that your invitations print as expected, run a quick test print before using your good paper.

Paperless Options

Let's be honest—we all get a little excited when a formal invitation arrives in the mail. However, your budget or timeline may not allow you the luxury of a traditional invitation, or you may be looking for a way to go green.

The ultimate way to go green is to send electronic invitations. However, while paperless invitations can be the cheapest and easiest option, they may not be practical or appropriate for your party. If your event does not call for a formal invitation, by all means take advantage of this inexpensive/free alternative. You will, however, only be able to invite those who actively use email, which means you will have to call, or send smoke signals to your Great-Aunt Gertrude.

When selecting the best paperless invitation option for your party, be mindful of how public your invitation, guest list, and any guest comments will be. For certain parties, it may be appropriate to hide your guest list or prohibit guests from posting comments. If you do allow guests to post comments, it is always a good idea to monitor the comments, in case a guest asks a question or offers to bring something to the party.

The list of paperless invitation options continues to grow. A simple Google search will give you a list of the newest sites you can use. Here is the list of three of the most popular online invitation options:

Evite (www.evite.com)

- ☐ It is free, easy to use, and saves your contact list for future use.

- ☐ If you don't find the perfect design in the countless options offered, you can upload your own picture or graphic.

☐ It is super easy to track RSVPs and see who has viewed your invitation.

☐ You can share your invitation on Facebook.

Paperless Post (www.paperlesspost.com)

☐ While not free, it is very inexpensive.

☐ All invitations are very elegant and appear very "real" — you can even add envelope lining.

☐ They offer an extensive selection of designs and allow you to customize nearly everything.

Facebook (www.facebook.com)

☐ It is free, although you and all of your guests must have Facebook accounts.

☐ If you do not mark your event "private," everyone on Facebook will be able to view your event details.

☐ You do not have invitation-style options, but you are able to add your own images.

Invitation Logistics

Once you have chosen either a traditional or paperless invitation, it is time to think about invitation logistics—wording, addressing/mailing, and RSVPs. Aside from the style of your invitation, your chosen wording and addressing style are the only ways for your guests to know how casual or formal your party will be.

Wording

If you have chosen a fill-in-the-blank invitation, you don't need to worry about wording, since that has been taken care of for you. For all other styles of invitations, you'll need to do a little work. Don't worry—there are endless invitation wording resources out there. You just need to know where to look. If the local stationery store or website you are purchasing the invitations from has not suggested wording that you like, simply search on the Web for your party type + "invitation wording" (i.e., "surprise 30th birthday invitation wording").

Don't be afraid to get creative or even a little goofy with your invitation wording, if appropriate—have a little fun with it! You may also be able to tie your party theme into your invitation wording. For example, if you are hosting a cooking shower, you can say:

- Come help us spice things up
- Let's spice up Kim and Steve's pantry

For most invitations, you will want to include response information. This is particularly important if you need to provide the caterer or venue a final headcount a week or two prior to the event. Even if you are not required to provide anyone with a final headcount, you will need to know how many guests to plan for. You can choose to ask all guests to respond "RSVP" or "the favor of a reply is requested." Or you may request "Regrets Only." In either case, it is helpful if you include a phone number as well as an email address so that guests may contact you in whatever method is most convenient for them. Be sure to include a "respond by" date if you need to make final arrangements for your event.

Addressing

It is very important to address your invitations appropriately so that your guests know who is and is not invited to the party. For example, if you address the invitation to "The Walkers," you should expect Mom, Dad, and all three kids. Conversely, if you address the invitation to "John and Sara Walker," they will know that they need to find a babysitter for the evening. Unfortunately you will need to brace yourself for guests who call to ask if they can bring their uninvited little ones, or even worse, those who simply show up with their children (yikes!).

If at all possible, take the time to hand-address all of your invitations or enlist the help of a friend—it really doesn't take very long. If you must use printed labels, be sure to use a legible font.

If you are having trouble determining how to address an invitation to your aunt who is a doctor and her live-in boyfriend, simply refer to one of the invitation websites in our "shop online" section for advice. If you are not able to find an answer there, search for "addressing wedding invitations." You'll find that many of your unique party planning issues and questions can be answered on wedding websites. After all, weddings are the ultimate party!

After you have addressed all of your invitations, don't forget to add a return address. If you decided to splurge and have your return address printed on the invitation envelopes, this has already been done for you. Whether you use return address labels, a stamp, or an embosser, make sure it is legible and adds to the style of your invitation. Keep in mind that your invitation is your guest's first glimpse of your event.

Mailing

Now that your invitations are addressed, it is time to throw a stamp on them and drop them in the mail! Yes, this is yet another opportunity to style your invitation. Once you have determined how much postage is required to mail your invitations (square invitations often cost more to mail), spend the time picking a complimentary stamp if you can. You may find that the post office is offering cartoon character stamps that are perfect for the first birthday party invitations you are sending. You may also want to create custom stamps with the guest of honor's picture or an ultrasound picture on them. They are a bit more expensive but super cute and one of a kind. However, don't fret if your only option is a standard stamp.

When deciding the appropriate time to mail your invitations, you should take into account the time of year and how formal the event is. Most invitations should be mailed three to six weeks in advance of your event to allow guests adequate time to respond, make any necessary childcare arrangements, and ensure that they do not already have plans. For example, if you are throwing a spring birthday party, mailing the invitations three weeks before the party is sufficient. However, if you are throwing a large Christmas party, you will want to mail your invitations much earlier to allow guests enough time to adjust their schedules during that busy time of year.

RSVPs

It is never too early to start thinking about how you will keep track of guest RSVPs. After all, you will likely receive your first responses within two days of mailing your invitations. Tracking RSVPs as they come in is important, because it is easy to lose track of who called two days ago. You will either underestimate the number of guests you will have or think that a guest never responded.

I find that it is easiest to track RSVPs in the same spreadsheet that you used to create your address list. By tracking all guest information in the same spreadsheet, you can easily put together a list of guests for personalized favors, place cards, or a thank-you note address list for the guest of honor.

If you are expecting all of your RSVPs by phone, you may find it is easier to use the address list you printed to address the invitations. You can simply check off the guests as they reply.

Decorations

Now it is time to get creative and take your theme to the next level! It is easy to translate your party theme into decorations that fit any budget. If you have chosen a common theme or one which is very popular, you won't have any trouble finding everything from plates and napkins to centerpieces and balloons. If, however, you have chosen a unique theme, don't fret. It is easy to give your party a coordinated and unified feel by simply using core colors or styles throughout all of your decorations. For example, if you have chosen a "Banana Split" theme for a summer get-together, use white, brown, and pink decorations to represent vanilla, chocolate, and strawberry ice cream, and throw in a few bananas for good measure.

It is also easy to create functional decorations by using the gifts you have purchased for the guest of honor or items found around the house that coordinate with your theme. For instance, if you are throwing a pool party, use beach towels for tablecloths, and hang a few beach balls from your light fixtures. See how easy, inexpensive, and fun decorating can be! If you have room in your budget, by all means, go all out!

Where to Find Decorations

If you are not planning to make your own decorations, it is time to start shopping! Here are some of my favorite places to find great party decorations:

☐ Your local stationery, craft, or party store

☐ A "big box" retailer like Target or Wal-Mart

☐ Online

- www.etsy.com
- www.orientaltrading.com
- www.acmepartybox.com
- www.partycity.com
- www.birthdayexpress.com
- www.shindigz.com

Favors

Party favors are a fun extension of your party theme and a great way to commemorate your event. They are also a nice way to thank your guests for coming. Favors are by no means required, so if your budget is tight or you don't have the time, this is not a deal breaker. Do, however, understand that guests will likely expect to receive favors at birthday parties and showers.

You will likely come across a lot of favor ideas when you are doing the legwork to choose your theme and decorations. Bookmark those websites or keep an "ideas" file to go back to when it is time to pick your favors. Keep in mind that it is easy to personalize just about any favor by adding a cute sticker that coordinates with your party theme. Favors are the most fun when they are a creative extension of your party theme. For example, give out a gift bag filled with Cracker Jacks, peanuts, and Double Bubble at a World Series party.

There are a lot of fun ways to make your favors do double duty by making them part of your décor or entertainment. Above all else, make sure your favors are fun, functional, or edible. For small children, stick to books, healthy low-sugar snacks, or practical toys and crafts—parents will thank you! There is almost nothing worse than leaving a party with a favor that you are just going to throw in the donation pile, or worse, the trash. Don't forget to place the favors near the door, so guests do not forget to take one with them.

Favors That Can Do Double Duty As Décor

- ☐ Personal place card holders
- ☐ Cookie cutter used as a napkin ring
- ☐ Small bud vases with a single flower
- ☐ A candy buffet that allows guests to make their own favor bags
- ☐ Small boxes (or any favor that can be stacked) arranged on a cake stand as your table centerpiece
- ☐ Lightweight favors hung from a clothesline with cute clothespins

Making your own favors can be easy and a lot of fun if you have the time (and can also save you a bundle). It's easy to find inspiration for making your own favors by searching the top favor websites. If you don't have the time or aren't crafty, there are a lot of places to buy party favors. You can find favors on all of the highlighted party websites or these top wedding favor websites:

- www.beau-coup.com
- www.littlethingsfavors.com
- www.favorsbyserendipity.com

Entertainment

How will you entertain all of the wonderful guests you have lured to your party with your perfect invitations and highly anticipated theme? If you have dotted all of your i's and crossed your t's, you should expect guests to arrive anticipating a fabulous party. To decide on the type of entertainment you will have, you should first take your theme and guest list into consideration. If possible, your entertainment should enhance your party theme and must be appropriate for your guests. For example, you do not want to play a word search game with three-year-olds, even if it is perfect for your party theme.

Party Games

Party games are not just for showers, and they definitely do not have to be boring and cheesy. Party games come in two varieties: active and passive. An active party game is one that everyone actively participates in together, such as, "How would the bride complete this sentence?" or hitting a piñata. Passive games, on the other hand, are usually set up where guests can participate if they choose at their leisure, such as signing a signature mat for a couple's engagement picture. Whether you choose an active or passive game, it is important to tie the game into your party theme if you can (i.e., a blind barbeque sauce taste test at your summer backyard barbeque).

Active Party Games

☐ Baby bottle bowling at a sports-themed first birthday

☐ Treat-filled piñata at a pool party

☐ Can the bride finish the groom's sentence? At a bridal shower

Passive Party Games

☐ Advice cards for the parents-to-be at a baby shower

☐ A list of must see movies at a Hollywood 10th birthday

☐ Guess the score at halftime at a Super Bowl party

Music

Livening up a party, or simply creating ambiance, is very easy to do with music. Having music at your party can be as easy as turning on the radio or as involved as hiring a DJ or a band. If you decide to splurge on a DJ or a band, the easiest way to find the best acts in your area is to search for local wedding vendors or to ask a friend.

If you are simply looking for background music, there are a number of free options.

Easy Ways to Play Background Music at Your Party

☐ Turn on a radio in a central location or create a party playlist on your iPod and dock it in a speaker stand. If you have an intercom system, take advantage of it!

☐ Download an Internet radio app (such as Pandora) to your smart phone or laptop, or play your satellite radio.

Eat, Drink, and Have a Party!

Your menu is yet another extension of your party theme—it may even be the cornerstone of your theme. Whether you are hosting a cocktail party potluck or catering a four-course dinner, have fun picking out foods that your guests will enjoy. You will have even more fun picking your menu if the food is part of your theme, such as a holiday cookie baking party, a hot fudge sundae birthday party or a cookies and milk adoption shower.

Things to Keep in Mind When Picking a Menu

- ☐ Food allergies/preferences (vegan, vegetarian). Label food to avoid any unfortunate mishaps.

- ☐ Finger foods don't require utensils but will require extra napkins.

- ☐ If you are serving food on a buffet that requires utensils, make sure you have adequate seating for your guests.

- ☐ Have both alcoholic and non-alcoholic options available for your guests.

Let's Eat!

When selecting what food to serve at your party, it is important to take into consideration how the food will be served. If you are hosting an Oscar party at home and have limited space to set up a buffet, consider serving mainly finger foods that require less space and can be displayed on two- and three-tier serving trays. If you are hosting a formal birthday party in the private room of a local restaurant, consider choosing a menu that provides guests with multiple main course options.

Food Service Options

- ☐ Buffet
  - ▪ Keep all of your serving dishes full, and clear any empty dishes.
  - ▪ Ensure that hot food stays hot and cold food stays cold.
  - ▪ Place the appropriate serving utensils in each dish.
  - ▪ Label dishes to avoid any confusion or possible allergic reactions.
- ☐ Passed appetizers
  - ▪ Have plenty of napkins with each passed platter.
  - ▪ Consider giving guests plates in lieu of handing them appetizers on napkins.
  - ▪ Ensure that those passing the appetizers know what each item is to avoid any allergy mishaps.
  - ▪ Pass multiple platters of the same appetizer at least twice.
- ☐ Sit-down dinner
  - ▪ Allow adequate time for your guests to arrive and mingle prior to serving the first course.
  - ▪ Ensure that the table is set with all necessary flatware, glassware, and condiments.
  - ▪ Clear any used dishes in between courses.
  - ▪ Allowing time between dinner and dessert allows additional time for guests to mingle and provides adequate time to make coffee or warm dessert.

Be sensitive to your guests' dietary restrictions and serve a variety of food so that your vegetarian friends are not stuck eating only carrot sticks. It is always good to have munchies that are placed in a location separate from the main food display, so guests are able to grab a quick snack. Whenever possible, it is good to have backup snacks in case you run out of food or have a few unexpected guests. Don't worry, this does not mean ordering twice the food you think you need it means having an extra box of crackers and cheese spread or a box of cookies, just in case.

When deciding on what food to serve at your party, you are not simply deciding between cooking everything yourself or hiring a caterer—there are countless options in between.

Food Options

- ☐ Cook everything yourself.
- ☐ Provide the main course and ask guests to bring their favorite side dish.
- ☐ Buy party trays from your local wholesale club or grocery store.
- ☐ Order take-out trays or have food delivered from your favorite restaurant.
- ☐ Buy premade meals from your local grocery store.
- ☐ Hire a caterer.

When setting your menu, do not forget about desserts, cake, or cupcakes. If you are lucky, you may have a go-to bakery in your neighborhood where you get all of your confections. If not, check your local grocery store or wholesale club, or ask friends for recommendations. Yelp.com is a great resource for finding local recommendations. If you are having a party for little ones or one that includes them, remember to have a kid-friendly dessert that is the appropriate portion size and not too difficult to eat (without making a mess).

Cake is and has always been the go-to dessert for most parties—you cannot go wrong with a cake. It is, however, fun to have a variety of cupcakes, a few pies, an assortment of cookies, or a chocolate fountain. As with everything at your party, try to get a little creative, tie your dessert back to your party theme, or both! Just don't forget to preorder your dessert or allow enough time to bake your own.

Raise Your Glass!

Raise your glass! Whether you are having a cocktail party or throwing an alcohol-free event, setting your drink menu is fun! Like your food menu, it is important to have a variety of drink options for your guests. No matter what type of party you are throwing, you always need to have water available. Other than that, your options are seemingly endless.

A fun way to start your drink menu is by selecting a "signature drink" to personalize your party. A "signature drink" can also be more economical than a variety of drinks because you are serving a large quantity. Your "signature drink" does not have to be alcoholic—it just has to be fun! This is yet another area where you can get creative and come up with your own drink recipe or a fun name. Consider naming your drink based on your party theme or after your guest of honor, like "Colin's Cocoa" (chocolate milk served at Colin's "Milk & Cookies" second birthday party).

Signature Drink Ideas

- ☐ Alcoholic
  - Berry champagne punch
  - White wine sangria

- Pomegranate martini
- Pineapple-orange mimosa
- Hazelnut Irish coffee

☐ Non-Alcoholic
- Strawberry pink lemonade
- Passion fruit tea
- Orange water
- Raspberry sherbet punch
- Peppermint hot chocolate

Non-Alcoholic Drink Options

☐ Soda (regular, diet, and caffeine-free)

☐ Juice (consider juice boxes for little ones)

☐ Water
- Ice water
- Flavored water (just add cucumber slices, fresh mint leaves, orange or lemon slices, etc., to a pitcher of water)

Alcoholic Drink Options

☐ Beer (domestic, imported, craft, or local brew)

☐ Wine (red, white, and sparkling)

☐ Mixed drinks

☐ Blender drinks

Whether you are serving a "signature drink" or not, or alcohol or not, it is good to have a variety of beverages for your guests to choose from. When you are calculating how many drinks to have on hand, remember that guests will drink an average of two drinks the first hour and one drink each hour after that. If the weather is hot, count on your guests drinking a bit more. You will also want to take your guest list into consideration—if your guests are big drinkers, have extra drinks on hand. It is always better to have too much than too little.

Setting up your drinks in a fun way can also add to the style and theme of your party, so have fun with it! If you are having a casual backyard barbeque, blow up a small inflatable pool and fill it with ice and cold drinks. For a more formal bridal shower, you can mimic your buffet table setup and post a drink menu for an added personal touch. Whether your party is casual or formal, it will save you time and numerous explanations if you include labels in your drink setup, such as an index card on top of each cooler listing the types of beer or an "Orange Sherbet Punch" card displayed in front of your punch bowl.

Drink Must-Haves

- ☐ Glassware
  - ▪ Go green and use your own glassware instead of plastic cups.
  - ▪ Use reusable plastic cups or shatterproof cups if you are worried about breaks.
  - ▪ Have kid-friendly cups on hand for little ones.
- ☐ Set out coasters to protect your furniture.
- ☐ Set glass markers next to glasses, so guests can tell their glasses apart.
  - ▪ Put a piece of painter's tape on each glass and leave a few markers on the table for guests to write their names or draw a cute picture.

☐ Have a variety of options available if you are serving cans or bottles.

▪ Have a recycling center set up for disposing of cans and bottles.

Party Timeline

A key part of party logistics is mapping out your party timeline. When will food be served? When will you play games? When will the cake be cut? It is important to give this some thought prior to the big day, so you are not scrambling during the party or forget to cut the cake! While it is important to outline your timeline, it is just as important to go with the flow, just in case you need to make any last-minute adjustments based upon the actual flow of the party. If, for example, you sense that the energy level at your party is waning, it may be time to start one of your activities. Or, if guests are having a wonderful time chatting, you may decide to skip one of your planned activities.

A party should be fun and allow adequate time for guests to mingle and eat without feeling rushed. When drafting your party timeline, you need to take into consideration the type of party you are having: the location, planned entertainment, your menu, your guests, etc. Every party timeline is as unique as your party; the good news is that the order of events is usually the same. Here are a few sample timelines to help you get started:

"Something Old and Something New" Bridal Shower

☐ 1–2:15 PM: guests arrive, mingle, and eat

☐ 2:15–2:30 PM: play shower game

☐ 2:30 –3 PM: open gifts

☐ 3–3:30 PM: serve cake/cupcakes, mingle, and snack

"End of Summer" Backyard Cookout

☐ 5–5:30 PM: guests arrive, grab a drink and snack

☐ 5–6:30 PM: play the backyard games you set up beforehand

☐ 6 PM: turn on the grill and start cooking!

☐ 6:30 PM: serve dinner

☐ 7–8 PM: play backyard games or move inside if the light has faded

☐ 7:30 PM: serve dessert

"ABCs and Me!" First Birthday Party

☐ 11–11:15 AM: little ones arrive

☐ 11 AM–12:30 PM: play games, start activities

☐ 12:30–1:15 PM: serve lunch (be prepared for a mess!)

☐ 1:15 PM: serve cake/cupcakes

☐ 1:30 PM: open gifts if the little one is up to it. If not, play more games!

2

Planning with Co-Hostesses

Planning a party with a co-hostess(es) can make planning easier, cheaper, and even more fun, but it does require additional planning and coordination. Just like managing a project team at work, it is very important to set expectations and assign responsibilities before you start planning. The easiest way to start a group planning process is to schedule an initial meeting with all of the hostesses. If you have the luxury of meeting with the other ladies in person, take the time to meet over a cup of coffee or invite them to your home one evening. If coordinating everyone's busy schedule is a little too taxing, get creative! You can just as easily coordinate via email, conference call, or Skype. A quick Skype video chat over your lunch hour will allow you to answer the initial pressing questions and kick off the planning process.

Preplanning Questions

☐ Will each hostess share in the party expenses?

☐ Will you collectively set a party budget (and stick to it)?

☐ Will you divide up certain responsibilities?

Once you have determined if a budget will be set and split, and if responsibilities will be shared, it is time to start divvying up those planning responsibilities. You will follow the same Clueless Chick planning processes, with one exception—you don't have to do everything yourself. When determining who is going to handle each aspect of the party, be sure to leverage everyone's individual strengths and availability. It is also helpful if you are able to group similar responsibilities. For instance, the hostess who will be purchasing and mailing the invitations is likely best suited to track RSVPs, while the hostess responsible for decorations is likely best suited to purchase coordinating paper products.

Above all else, it is important to communicate with your co-hostesses and track everything. You can easily accomplish these goals by leveraging online collaboration tools such as Google Docs to maintain all party documentation, such as:

☐ Contact list

☐ Budget

☐ Responsibilities

☐ Purchases

☐ Reimbursements

As the date of the party nears, you will need to touch base more frequently to ensure that everything is on track and to hand off any last-minute duties. On the day of the party, as you are running around setting everything up and taking care of the endless last-minute details, you will be very thankful that you did not do all of this work alone!

When Planning with Co-Hostesses Is a Good Idea

- ☐ You are throwing a very large wedding shower that would be cost-prohibitive without additional help.

- ☐ You are throwing a baby shower and the mommy-to-be's sister-in-law from out of state really wants to contribute.

- ☐ Your best friend is planning a surprise 50th birthday party for her husband but clearly needs some help.

- ☐ You are planning a large event, which includes guests from multiple social circles, and you would like to include a hostess from each circle.

A unique twist on a co-hostess: you may find yourself working with a co-hostess who is a hostess in name only, much like a silent business partner. This may be the bride's future mother-in-law or the mommy-to-be's great aunt, who would like to make a financial contribution to the event but is not involved in the planning details.

3

Party Etiquette

As with most everything in life, there is a "right" way and a "wrong" way to host a party, be a great guest, and be a great guest of honor. Whether you successfully completed Junior Cotillion or have no earthly idea why a place setting includes two forks, there are a few etiquette musts that will get you through almost any situation. Why is it important to consider appropriate etiquette when planning your party? If you are sensitive to local etiquette, customs, and traditions, all of your party guests will be comfortable. It is also just as important to know your guests and to be sensitive to whether or not they are familiar with etiquette norms. For example, you may have guests who do not RSVP as requested, and you will simply have to contact them directly. I believe we should always lead by example, but we should never intentionally make someone feel uncomfortable if she is not familiar with the most appropriate way to handle a social situation. It may be important to let certain things go—which may be easier said than done (not that I would know anything about that!).

If you are unsure of how to handle a unique situation involving your party, how to address your invitations, or are simply interested in getting an expert's advice, here are a few of my favorite etiquette resources:

- ☐ www.emilypost.com
- ☐ www.missmanners.com
- ☐ www.elaineswann.com

There are plenty of additional online resources, blogs, and books at your local bookstore. When you are citing an etiquette source, please ensure that it is a reputable source! Don't be like Patrick Dempsey in *Can't Buy Me Love,* who performed the African anteater ritual at the prom.

If you are having a hard time finding answers to your party etiquette questions, try searching wedding websites—again, a wedding *is* the ultimate party.

Tips for Being a Great Hostess

With these few simple tips and tricks, you are sure to be renowned as the "Hostess with the Mostess!"

- ☐ Address invitations appropriately, and send them out well in advance of the event to allow ample time for guests to reply and make arrangements to attend.

- ☐ Be conscious of who you are inviting. If you are throwing a stock-the-bar party, you may not want to invite your friends who do not drink.

☐ Arrange additional help before the party if you need an extra set of hands to set up, clean up, or watch the kids. When in doubt, see if the teenager down the street is interested in helping for a few extra bucks.

☐ Greet guests when they arrive. If you are unavoidably detained, ensure that someone is there to greet guests at the door.

☐ Offer guests something to eat or drink as soon as you have taken their coat and bag.

☐ Take the time to chat with each of your guests throughout the event, and introduce guests to those they have not met before.

☐ Thank your guests as they leave and make sure they have their coats and bags.

☐ Give your guest of honor a Clueless Chick post-party kit.

The Clueless Chick™ Post-Party Kit

☐ Thank-you notes

☐ Stamps

☐ Pen

☐ Party guest address list

☐ Completed gift register

☐ Party favor

☐ An extra invitation for her scrapbook

Tips for Being a Great Guest

Here are a few tips that are sure to put you at the top of everyone's guest list!

☐ Reply promptly to all invitations in the manner requested.

- If you misplace your invitation and do not have the hostess's contact information, ask the guest of honor for her phone number. Do not reply to the guest of honor—she should not be doing any work.

☐ Only those listed on your invitation are invited to the event.

- If the invitation was addressed to "Mr. and Mrs. Joe Wright," only the husband and wife are invited. Do not make the host uncomfortable by asking if she meant to invite your kids.
- If the invitation was addressed to "The Wright Family," the whole family is welcome to attend.
- If the invitation was addressed to a child, assume that one parent should attend as a chaperone unless the child is old enough to be dropped off.

☐ If something unavoidable arises after you have replied, call the hostess immediately to explain the situation.

☐ If you cannot find a sitter, send your regrets and a gift or note, if appropriate.

☐ Take a small hostess gift such as flowers, a bottle of wine, a picture frame, or a serving piece as a token of your gratitude.

☐ If you loved the event, let the host know by writing her a short note or sending a quick email. People appreciate recognition for all of the hard work they put into an event.

Tips for Being a Great Guest of Honor

The best way to thank your hostess for putting so much time and effort into throwing such a great party in your honor is to be a great guest of honor!

- ☐ Offer to help your host, even if you know she will not take you up on your offer.

- ☐ Ask if the host would like you to arrive at a special time.

- ☐ Thank your hostess by writing her a nice personal note or buying a small thank-you gift.

- ☐ Greet all of your guests and thank them for coming.

- ☐ Mingle! Make sure you have a chance to speak to everyone and introduce friends from different social circles to one another.

- ☐ Promptly send thank-you notes for any gifts you received to thank your friends for their thoughtfulness.

4

Party Logistics

Logistics are key to a successful, enjoyable, and stress-free party. Just like a little planning can go a long way to easing your stress level, a well-organized party is more enjoyable for you and your guests. If you aren't a planner by nature, pick your battles; focus on the aspects of the party that are most important to you and let the rest go or outsource.

Party Setup Tips for The Clueless Chick™

When you are planning your party setup strategy, do not forget the four S's of setup: staging area, stations, storage, and simplify:

☐ Staging Area

- Create a staging area in an out-of-the-way (and out-of-sight) place, such as the laundry room, garage, or a closet, where you can stash extra food, containers, empty platters, etc.

- Make sure the dishwasher is empty before the party starts, so you can quickly and easily fill it with dirty dishes.

☐ Stations

- Create self-contained stations for food, drinks, activities, etc. Creating these designated areas will promote a natural flow and mingling during the party and prevent guests from needing to wander around trying to find a napkin when they are fixing a plate of food.

- Designate an area for guests to place gifts when they arrive. It is best if this is the same spot where gifts will be opened, so they do not have to be moved in the middle of the party. If, however, you will not be opening gifts during the party or are not expecting to receive gifts, put any gifts guests bring in another room, so as not to make other guests uncomfortable.

- Place trash receptacles in an easily accessible area and clearly label recycling and compost containers.

☐ Storage

- On a rainy day, have a bucket for wet umbrellas and an effective way to dry wet/muddy shoes.

- Designate an easily accessible area for coats, purses, diaper bags, etc.

☐ Simplify

- Wrapping silverware in a napkin makes it easier for guests to grab while they are fixing a plate of food and will encourage them to take only one set of flatware.

- Arrange seating so that guests do not need to move any furniture.

- Place coasters on all wood surfaces so that guests do not have to hunt for them.

- If you are expecting any babies or small children, make room for a diaper changing area and place a stool in the bathroom so that little ones can reach the sink.

- Plan how you will send leftovers home with guests so you are not scrambling at the end of the party.

- Consider placing favors by the door, so guests do not forget to take one.

And finally, the most important part of any setup: take pictures! Make sure you snap a few shots of your amazing handiwork before guests arrive.

Setting up at Home

One of the advantages of hosting a party at home is the ability to set up the day, or even the week, before the party. It is also easier to enlist extra help if you have more flexibility in your schedule.

The Day(s) before the Party

☐ Arrange furniture and serving pieces.

☐ Clean the house, or even better, find a cleaning service to come over the weekend before.

- ☐ Tell your neighbors if there will be a large number of cars parking around your neighborhood.
- ☐ Cook as much as you can ahead of time.

The Day of the Party

- ☐ If practical, place a few serving dishes somewhere other than the kitchen, so everyone is not crowded in the kitchen or around a single food table.
- ☐ Put any animals away, in case any guests have allergies.
- ☐ Set up trash cans and recycling bins.

Setting up on Location

- ☐ See how early the venue will let you begin setting up.
- ☐ Take full advantage of the space they give you.
- ☐ Ensure that your rented location has trash and recycling receptacles—if not, bring your own.
- ☐ Carry everything in big tubs. It makes for fewer trips and easier cleanup, and the tubs can easily be stored under a table or in the coat closet.

Party Cleanup Tips for The Clueless Chick™

Cleanup can be overwhelming, especially when you are tired from all of the prep work, setup, and hosting. By taking a little time to plan ahead, you can avoid a number of headaches and ensure that your cleanup goes quickly and as smoothly as possible. When you are planning your party cleanup strategy, do not forget the four C's of cleanup: continuous, coordinated, careful, and consolidate:

☐ Continuous

- Clean as you go! If you can take a minute to pick up a dirty dish or put away an item no longer in use, you will save yourself time and make cleanup seem less daunting at the end of the party.

- Towards the end of the party, look through your storage area to ensure that no one has forgotten a coat, purse, etc.

☐ Coordinated

- Enlist help. Ask a friend or relative to chip in, or hire a local teen to help for an hour or so.

- Make sure you have a way to carry gifts out to the guest of honor's car.

☐ Careful

- Walk the entire party space twice to ensure you've gotten everything.

- Make sure the recycling is suitable to dump into the recycling bin. Ensure that there isn't any recycling in your trash.

☐ Consolidate

- Move larger items to your staging area to get them out of the way.

- Quickly pack up leftovers by placing them back in their original packaging or prep/transport container.

Tips for Sending Leftovers Home

☐ When sending home an extra cupcake with a party guest, drop the cupcake into a plastic cup for easy transportation. If your guest doesn't mind the frosting getting a little messy (who does?!), you can also place a second cupcake upside down on top of the first.

☐ Simply drop dry foods such as cookies, breads, etc. into a zip-top bag for easy transport.

☐ Save heavy plastic take-out containers to pack leftovers in.

☐ Wrap any messy leftovers in tin foil.

☐ Have a few bags on hand in case guests are carrying multiple to go containers.

Cleanup at Home:

When you are hosting a party at your home, you have the luxury of taking your time to clean up, unless you are like me and must have everything back in its place as soon as possible. Here are a few additional tips to help you quickly and easily clean up after a party at home, so you can finally put your feet up and relax:

☐ Put as many dirty dishes as you can into the dishwasher.

☐ Throw away any trash that is left out.

☐ If you have been drinking, do not wash your good wine glasses or any other fragile dishes—they can wait until the morning.

Tips for party planners who will wait until the next morning to clean up:

☐ Wrap up/refrigerate any food you want to keep or donate (or don't want the ants to visit overnight).

☐ Leave dishes in the sink to soak in soapy water, so you are not faced with a dried-on mess.

Cleanup on Location:

Ideally, if you are paying to have your party at a special location, they will clean up for you! If not, or if you are having the party at a park or other unmanned location, here are the cleanup tips you can't live without:

☐ Bring bags that you can easily throw everything into if you are in a hurry.

☐ Throw everything back in the large tubs you carried everything in with.

☐ Verify when you need to be out of a rented space, and plan accordingly.

☐ Collect any items you want to keep, such as gift bags, tissue paper, and ribbon. This is especially important if you are hosting a bridal shower and need to make a ribbon bouquet.

5

Go Green!

When you are trying to go green, every little bit helps. A few easy changes during your planning process can go a long way in reducing your party's carbon footprint.

On the following pages are a few of my favorite Go Green tips.

Green Party Planning Checklist
for The Clueless Chick™

☐ Event
_____

☐ Date
_____

☐ Time   Choose a time of day that requires the least amount of energy, such as mid-day, when you will not need to turn on all of the lights in your home and can open windows for a cool breeze.

☐ Guest Count
_____

☐ Budget
_____

☐ Theme   Choose a theme that challenges guests to Go Green. Offer a prize to the guest who was most creative in their effort to go green.

☐ Location   Choose a location that does not have a negative impact on the environment and is centrally located so guests do not have to travel far or are able to carpool/take public transportation.

☐ Invitations   Choose a paperless invitation option. If you need to send a formal invitation, choose the highest post-consumer recycled content you can find.

☐	Decorations	Use your gifts for the guest of honor as decorations.
		▪ Hang baby clothes on a clothes line for a baby shower.
		▪ Use the crystal vase from the registry wrapped in a large cello bag as a table centerpiece.
		▪ Create a kitchen utensil arrangement for a cooking shower.
☐	Favors	Make your favors do double duty as decorations.
		▪ Cookie cutters used as napkin rings.
		▪ Small bud vases with a single flower.
		▪ A candy buffet that allows guests to make their own favor bags (a bit overdone but still fun).
		▪ Lightweight favors from a clothesline with cute clothespins.
		Or skip favors all together.
☐	Entertain-ment	Create a fun activity with items you already have around the house, such as playing musical chairs at a kid's birthday party.
☐	Menu	
	Food	Avoid serving food that requires additional packaging.
		Serve a menu of locally grown foods.
	Drinks	Skip the bottled water—put ice water in a large jug or drink dispenser.
		Purchase drinks in large containers as opposed to individual servings.

☐ Timeline

☐ Paper
Products

Get biodegradable disposable items
—napkins, plates, etc.

- Set up recycling and compost
  stations, and tell a few key guests
  about it, so they can help point
  other guests in the right direction.

- Invest in serving dishes and skip
  the plastic disposable ones.

- Using real dishes and flatware will
  encourage people to only use one
  set and will significantly reduce
  waste.

- In the summertime, use Mason jars
  to serve lemonade.

☐ Gifts

Ask guests to skip wrapping paper/
gift bags/tissue paper and wrap their
gifts in the Sunday funny pages or a
reusable shopping bag

- Save gift wrapping, bags, etc. to be
  reused.

6

Party Planning on a Budget

Even on the tightest of budgets, you can throw a fabulously unforgettable party! When you are setting your budget, watch out for the infamous budget busters.

Budget Busters

- ☐ Food and drinks
- ☐ Location
- ☐ Entertainment
- ☐ Decorations
- ☐ Favors
- ☐ Invitations

Here are a few easy ways to keep budget busters under control:

Party Budget for the Budget-Conscious Clueless Chick

☐ Location and
  Coordination

Location Rental Fee	Choose a non-peak day and time to lower venue rental fees.
	Have your party at home, or choose an inexpensive or free location, such as your local park or public pool.
Rentals	Choose a location that includes tables, chairs, lines, etc.

☐ Party Planner | Choose a location that includes an event coordinator.

☐ Invitations and Adornments | In lieu of a traditional invitation, choose a paperless option or create your own invitation with craft supplies you already have.

☐ Postage

☐ Decorations | Buy only a few key decorations to match your theme (i.e., one Barbie balloon surrounded by four pink and purple balloons) and purchase everything else in coordinating solid colors, which are much less expensive.

  ▪ Shop the clearance rack to piece together eclectic decorations—it is fun and funky.

- The dollar store is your friend! You would be surprised how much you can find there.
- Make your own funky decorations with items you already have around the house.
- Use beach towels for tablecloths.
- Set up your little one's toys as centerpieces at a baby shower.

☐ Favors   Make favors like cookies, Rice Crispies treats, or homemade crafts.

Make your favors do double duty as decorations.

- Cookie cutters used as napkin rings
- Small bud vases with a single flower
- A candy buffet that allows guests to make their own favor bags (a bit overdone but still fun)
- Lightweight favors hung from a clothesline with cute clothespins
- Skip favors all together

☐ Entertainment

☐ Music   Set up your iPod, satellite, or Internet radio to play music.

☐ Games   Play games you can create with items you already have around the house

Baby bottle bowling at a first birthday party.

☐ Menu

Food	Pick a time of day when guests will not expect a full meal, such as early afternoon.
	Prepare all of the food yourself.
	Serve light appetizers.
	Host a potluck/covered dish party and ask guests to bring a favorite side dish.
	Set up an evite that allows guests to pick a dish to bring.
	Base your menu on current grocery store sales or local deals.
	Have a bagel pizza party on the day your local bagel shop offers a dozen bagels for $4.99.
	Purchase large party platters from your local discount club or grocery store.
Drinks	Serve a variety of flavored water (cucumber, orange, lemon, basil, etc.).
	Skip the alcohol.
	Invite guests to BYOB.
☐ Paper Products	
☐ Tableware (plates, napkins, flatware)	Use your own dishes in lieu of purchasing paper products.
	Instead of disposable plastic tablecloths, get a real tablecloth that can be washed and reused—you'll find that after two to three uses you have actually saved money.
☐ Glassware	

☐	Labor (setup/ cleanup, food service, babysitter, etc.)	Recruit a friend or family member to help.
☐		
☐		
	Total	$

7

Sample Parties

Showers

Bridal showers and baby showers are always so special because they are celebrating an extremely important event in the guest of honor's life. When planning a shower, remember that your party will end up in a photo album/scrapbook/keepsake box that will likely be passed down to the next generation. No pressure!

Top Five Shower Tips

1. Date: Choose a date that is not too close to the main event to ensure that the guest of honor can properly enjoy her shower.

2. Theme: Be sure that you are not giving away any wedding or baby secrets or forgetting an important custom or tradition with your chosen theme.

3. Guest list: If this is the only planned bridal or baby shower, the guest list may be quite long. Consider enlisting a co-hostess.

4. Entertainment: Get creative—avoid the overplayed and tacky shower games.

5. Special guests: Do not forget to include/acknowledge the guest of honor's mother/mother-in-law, as appropriate.

Bridal Shower Tips

Bridal showers are so much fun and the perfect time for the bride to be the center of attention without the pressures of the big day. You also have the opportunity at a bridal shower to give guests a sneak preview of the wedding, with the bride's permission, of course. For example, if they will be serving strawberry mojitos at the reception as their signature drink, you can serve strawberry pink lemonade at the bridal shower.

Bridal Shower Note: If this is the bride or groom's second go of it, you will need to be sensitive to what type of shower the bride would like; she may be looking forward to a traditional shower, or she may prefer to have a smaller "Girl's Day Out." In either case, this is an event to be celebrated!

Baby Shower Tips

Celebrating the impending arrival of a little bundle of joy is such an exciting time! Baby showers also require a bit of extra planning to accommodate a mommy-to-be's dietary restrictions. If you are not familiar with what foods are and are not safe during pregnancy, do a little online research or speak with an experienced friend. A fun way to work around pregnancy "don'ts" is to serve alcohol-free mocktails!

Sprinkle Tips

What's a "Sprinkle?" A sprinkle is a "lite" shower to celebrate baby No. 2 or No. 10! Mommy-to-be may have all of the baby gear and baby basics she needs from baby No. 1, so you can get creative with your theme! You may want to have a "Turning Blue Pink" shower to make all of her baby boy things girlie, a "Disposables" shower to restock her supply of diapers, wipes, creams, etc., or a "Mommy" theme to celebrate Mom and shower her with gifts.

Adoption Shower Tips

Welcoming a baby into his or her forever family with an adoption shower is an amazing experience. It is important not to under-estimate how emotional an adoption shower can be if the baby's arrival has been anticipated for years. While you will not have to make special adjustments to accommodate a pregnancy diet, you may need to accommodate a precious little newborn, which might mean that you do not invite any small children. If the state(s) involved in the adoption process have a revocation pe-riod, you may consider waiting until that time has elapsed before throwing a shower. To ensure that the baby has everything she needs upon arrival, consider having a "Post Paperwork" shower to shower Mommy with the bare necessities or arrange for her to borrow everything she needs as soon as the baby arrives.

Shower Party Checklist
for The Clueless Chick™

☐ Event | Lisa's Baby Shower

☐ Date | Saturday

☐ Time | 3 PM

☐ Guest Count | 20

☐ Budget | $300

☐ Theme | Pickles & Ice Cream

☐ Location | Home "Sweet" Home

☐ Invitations | Ice cream-shaped invitation with pickle confetti and ice cream cone sticker/ envelope closure

☐ Decorations | Tissue pom poms atop brown cardstock "cones"

Sweet and savory snacks served in ice cream dishes

☐ Favors | A cone-shaped cello bag filled with candies, tied with a pickle-shaped tag

☐ Entertainment | Blindfolded ice cream taste test

☐ Menu

Food | Ice cream sundae bar
Fun finger foods
Cupcakes baked in ice cream cones in lieu of cake

Drinks | Orange Sherbet Punch

☐ Timeline	3–4 PM: guests arrive, mingle, and eat
	4–4:30 PM: make ice cream sundaes and play shower game
	4:30–5 PM: open gifts
	5–5:30 PM: serve cupcakes, mingle, and snack
☐ Paper Products	Use your own dishes as well as the hodgepodge of ice cream dishes found at the discount store
	Purchase pickle-shaped napkins
☐	

Birthday Parties

Birthday parties are fun for kids of all ages! Whether you are throwing a 1st or 50th birthday party, you have the perfect opportunity to make your guest of honor feel like a king/queen for the day.

Birthday Party Tips

1. Menu: Be sensitive to allergies and dietary restrictions. If the guest of honor is diabetic, don't plan a dessert party.

2. Date: Choose a date that is most convenient for the guest of honor.

3. Theme: Make the theme as meaningful to the guest of honor as possible—after all, it is her special day.

4. Guest list: Be sensitive to how much people may talk about the birthday party. If you are having a kid's party, you do not want to pass out invitations at school unless you are inviting the whole class. The same may be true in the workplace, depending upon your circumstances.

5. Gifts: If you prefer that guests do not bring gifts, get creative! Avoid putting "no gifts" on the invitation. Instead, invite guests to "Please simply bring all of the hot air you can muster to help Ryan blow out his birthday candles," or schedule your party around a charity event.

Surprise Party Tips

Planning a surprise party on the sly to celebrate a milestone birthday, or as a huge thank you, is both fun and stressful. There are details you need to think of when planning a surprise party, such as whether everyone will be able to park out of the guest of honor's line of sight, or how you will get the guest of honor to the party location without her suspecting anything. It can also be a bit tricky to compile the guest list for a surprise party, so enlist the help of friends to ensure you are not forgetting anyone or including someone you shouldn't (images of a well-meaning mother planning a surprise 30th birthday party for her son by inviting everyone in his "little black book" flash through your head).

Kids' Party Tips

From 1st to 18th birthday parties, planning for a kid is tons of fun! It can also be a lot of work. Whoever said a house full of eight-year-olds was going to be a picnic? Unlike an adult party, kids will not simply "mingle." They require entertainment or structured activities, and it is nice to also have entertainment planned for any parents who will be attending the party with them. If parents won't be attending the party with their child, you may consider hiring your babysitter to lend a hand. Paying particular attention to your menu is also important to ensure that there are no mishaps with food allergies or dietary restrictions.

Grown-Up Party Tips

Just because we are over twenty-one doesn't mean we can't still have an awesome birthday party! A fun-filled grown-up birthday party is the perfect way to celebrate surviving another year or officially being one year closer to retirement. When you are creating your guest list, you will need to decide if you are going to include children; if you are, will you hire a babysitter for additional help? If you will be serving alcohol, you may also want to make arrangements with a local driving or cab service. A grown-up birthday party is also the perfect excuse for a day/ evening out; consider planning your party around a local sporting event, go-cart track, or spa.

Birthday Party Checklist
for The Clueless Chick™

☐	Event	Brent's 40th Birthday Party
☐	Date	Saturday
☐	Time	7 PM
☐	Guest Count	30
☐	Budget	$400
☐	Theme	Golf party
☐	Location	The Birthday Boy's home
☐	Invitations	A mock scorecard inviting guests to "Meet on the 18th green at 7 PM."
☐	Decorations	Golf movies and the Golf Channel playing on TV as background noise.

- Plan ahead and set the DVR to record the replay of a classic round of golf on the Golf Channel.
- Top golf movies: *Happy Gilmore, Caddy Shack, Legend of Bagger Vance, Greatest Game Ever Played.*
- Have golf visors and gloves for each of the guests to wear.

☐	Favors	A golf theme bag filled with golf tees and chocolate golf balls, tied with a "To the sweetest shot you've ever made" tag.
☐	Entertainment	Mini golf! Each guest uses a plastic toddler golf club and rubber plastic balls to play the course set up in the living room using plastic cups as holes.

Scores are registered on a large scorecard poster. The winner takes home a box of golf balls.

Purchase a golf towel or golf flag from his favorite course (or even better yet, have a personalized one made) for everyone to sign with a permanent fabric pen.

☐ Menu

Food

Edible golf clubs. Dip the top of a breadstick in chocolate, insert the bottom of the breadstick into a rectangular Rice Krispies treat (predrill a hole slightly smaller than the breadstick in the Rice Krispies treat so that neither piece breaks)

Heavy appetizers, each named after a famous golfer, or course, or term.

- "Birdie" chicken skewers
- "Pebble Beach" bean dip

Drinks

Arnold Palmer (sweet tea and lemonade)

John Daly (Firefly [sweet tea vodka] and lemonade)

☐ Timeline

7–8:15 PM: guests arrive, mingle, and eat

7:30–9:30 PM: play mini-golf

9:30 PM: announce mini-golf winner

9:30–10:30 PM: serve cake/cupcakes, mingle, and snack

☐ Gifts

Know his favorite brand of golf ball, driving range, and shirt size, should guests ask.

☐

Holiday Parties

Having a holiday party is a great way to celebrate a special occasion, be it the 4th of July or Christmas, with friends. Holiday parties are also the perfect way to bring together friends who are unable to travel home to spend the holiday with their families.

Top 5 Holiday Party Tips

1. Date and time: Consider planning your party a few days before or after the actual holiday, so that everyone can attend.

2. Customs: Know the traditional customs for the holiday, but have fun mixing them up a little.

3. Guest List: Consider including friends who do not necessarily celebrate the holiday to share your traditions with them (invite all of your American friends over for your Canada Day).

4. Decorations: Take advantage of the decorating you have already done for the holiday! Plan ahead and buy next year's decorations the day after the holiday when everything is fifty percentage off.

5. Menu: Serving a very traditional meal may bring back memories of celebrating at Grandma's house as a child.

Holiday Party Checklist
for The Clueless Chick™

☐ Event   Valentine's Brunch

☐ Date   Sunday

☐ Time   11 AM

☐ Guest Count   10

☐ Budget $150

☐ Theme   Valentine's Day

☐ Location   Love Shack

☐ Invitations   A box of conversation hearts with the invitation glued to the back.

- Invitations are printed at home on card stock, cut to size and glued to the box with a good old-fashioned glue stick. Boxes are then mailed to each guest in padded envelopes.
- Invitations also request that guests "Spread the love by bringing a stuffed animal to donate to charity."

☐ Decorations   Red and white Christmas lights (purchased at fifty percentage off the day after Christmas)

Red, pink, and white tissue puffs placed on the mantle, hung from light fixtures and around the front door.

Clear glass vases filled with Valentine's candies as centerpieces on the tables and buffet.

Place cards made with small paper Valentines.

☐ Favors	A single chocolate rose
☐ Entertainment	iPod with the ultimate love song playlist (with a few anti-love songs sprinkled in for good measure)
	"Worst Pickup Line Ever"
	Ask guests to write down the worst pickup line ever used on them, or the worst line they have ever used. Read all lines aloud (without revealing writers' names) and allow guests to vote on the winner. Award the winner a heart-shaped box of chocolates.
☐ Menu	
Food	My Little Muffin (mini muffins)
	Hot Cakes (heart-shaped pancakes)
	Me So EGGcited (scrambled eggs with onions and red peppers)
	Smokin' Hot Potatoes (home fries)
	What's Shakin' Bacon? (bacon strips)
	Stuck on You (sticky monkey bread)
	Sweet Tart (grapefruit halves, sugar)
	Chocolate fondue
Drinks	Love Potion #9 (red wine sangria)
	Friendship Potion #9 (strawberry pink lemonade)
☐ Timeline	11–11:30 AM: guests arrive and fill out Worst Pickup Line EVER card
	11:30 AM–1 PM: serve brunch
	12:30–1 PM: play Worst Pickup Line Ever
	1–2 PM: serve chocolate fondue

Theme Parties

Throwing a theme party can be as easy as having friends over to watch the Academy Awards, having an annual summer luau or hosting an authentic Kentucky Derby party.

Top 5 Theme Party Tips

1. Date and Time: Make sure you are planning around the correct date and time.

2. Guest list: Consider inviting many more guests than you anticipate hosting, assuming that many may have longstanding plans for the given event.

3. Costumes: Consider asking guests to come dressed for the occasion (fancy hats for a Derby party, or red-carpet ready for the Academy Awards).

4. Entertainment: Your main entertainment may be the purpose of the party; if not, find a fun game to complement your theme like a limbo at your summer luau.

5. Location: Choose a location that complements your theme, such as a private room at a sports bar for watching the Final Four.

Theme Party Checklist
for The Clueless Chick™

☐ Event   Super Bowl Bash

☐ Date   Super Bowl Sunday

☐ Time   One hour before kickoff

☐ Guest Count   25

☐ Budget $200

☐ Theme   Super Bowl

☐ Location   The Man Cave

☐ Invitations   Football-themed evite

☐ Decorations   As many TVs as you can find!

                     Nerf footballs, pom poms in team colors

                     Camping/tailgating chairs

                     Tailgating tent set up outside next to the grill

☐ Favors   Koozies

☐ Entertainment   Betting boards

- Super Bowl Squares for the length of the first drive to win the best seat in the house for the rest of the game
- Super Bowl Squares for the final score of the game to win a tailgating cooler
- Halftime "Guess the penalty" hand-signal game

☐ Menu

Food	Tailgate fare! Since most guests will be grabbing food during a commercial break and running back to their seats, everything should be easy run.

- Chips and dip
- Wings
- Burgers and hot dogs
- Veggies with ranch and hummus. Serve in plastic cups prefilled with ranch or hummus
- Cookies and brownies
- Snack mix served in football-themed favor cones

Drinks	Beer, soda, and bottled water stored in ice-filled tailgating coolers around the "Man Cave"

☐ Timeline

One hour before kickoff: guests begin to arrive and complete the betting squares

Kickoff: play "Length of the First Drive"

Halftime: play "Guess the Penalty"

After the game: determine betting squares winner

☐ _____

☐ _____

☐ _____

Everyday Get-Togethers

Who says you need a reason to throw a party? Even if you do not have a birthday, milestone, or event to celebrate, you can still throw a fabulous party! Whether you are planning a casual post-game barbeque or a formal dinner party, you can easily follow all of The Clueless Chick™ party planning steps and turn an everyday get-together into an unforgettable party.

Top 5 Everyday Get-Together Tips

1. Date and Time: Pick a date that will not conflict with any major events or celebrations (there is no rule that says you have to have your party on the weekend).

2. Invitations: Consider saving time, money, and effort by simply sending an email invitation that contains all of the event details.

3. Menu: Consider asking guests to bring a side dish.

4. Entertainment: Consider having a few board games on hand, in case anyone is interested in a round of Scene It.

5. Decorations: Having decorations is not a must for an everyday get-together, but it does help to pep up the experience.

Everyday Party Checklist
for The Clueless Chick™

☐	Event	Pool Party
☐	Date	Sunday
☐	Time	3 PM
☐	Guest Count	10
☐	Budget	$100
☐	Theme	Summer fun!
☐	Location	Neighborhood pool
☐	Invitations	email with all of the party details
☐	Decorations	Beach balls Beach blanket tablecloths Beach bucket filled with small water guns Beach bucket filled with containers of sunscreen (just in case) Kiddie pool filled with ice and drinks
☐	Favors	Beach balls and water guns—everyone takes one home!
☐	Entertainment	iPhone docked in a speaker stand playing the Pandora beach music channel Water balloon toss during swim breaks

☐ Menu

    Food | Small bunches of grapes, served in small beach buckets

                  Watermelon, served in a large beach bucket

                  Crackers and cheese

                  Veggie tray

                  Pita points and hummus, with a small shovel in lieu of a spoon

    Drinks | Water bottles and juice boxes in an ice filled inflatable pool

☐ Timeline | 3–3:30 PM: guests arrive

                  3–6 PM: swim and snack

☐ _____

☐ _____

☐ _____

Now What?

Now, go put all of your newfound knowledge to work! It is time to find your own inspiration and start planning. You have a lot of work ahead of you, but every bit of it is worth it when you see the looks on your guests' faces. The most important thing to remember is to have fun! Just remember to relax and enjoy every minute of the fabulous party you are about to throw.

For the latest tips and information about The Clueless Chick™, visit our website, www.CluelessChick.com. I hope you will keep coming back for more tips!

Until next time,

Jennifer

Origins of The Clueless Chick™

On June 30, 2009, my husband, Matt, and I were settling in for the night after putting our six-month-old to bed. Matt was telling me about another one of his brilliant book ideas, and I was only half paying attention. As he went on and on, it hit me that I needed to write a book! After all, I had just created a blog (www.justaskjennifer.blogspot.com) to collect all of my tips and tricks that people had been asking me to send them for years. If so many of my friends (and friends of friends) were interested in what I had to say, maybe I was on to something. The idea for The Clueless Chick™ series was born!

Matt and I immediately started brainstorming ideas and quickly determined that I would write a series of pocket guides for every woman, girlfriend, wife, and mother who would spend hours researching about all of life's milestones and obstacles, if she had more than five minutes to spare in her busy day. As the quintessential Type A/OCD overachiever, I can share all of my tips, tricks, and research to help point you in the right direction on your journey. I am here to clue you in!

Tear It Out and Take It with You

Party Planning Checklist for The Clueless Chick™

☐ Event   _____

☐ Date   _____

☐ Time   _____

☐ Guest count   _____

☐ Budget   _____

☐ Theme   _____

☐ Invitations   _____

☐ Decorations   _____

☐ Favors   _____

☐ Entertainment   _____

☐ Menu   _____

    Food   _____

    Drinks   _____

☐ Timeline   _____

☐   _____

☐   _____

Party Budget for The Clueless Chick™

☐ Location and coordination   _____

     Location rental fee   _____

     Rentals (tables, chairs,
     linens, etc.)   _____

     Party planner   _____

☐ Invitations   _____

     Invitations/Adornments   _____

     Postage   _____

☐ Decorations   _____

☐ Favors   _____

☐ Entertainment   _____

     Music   _____

     Games   _____

☐ Menu   _____

     Food   _____

     Drinks   _____

☐ Paper products   _____

     Tableware (plates, napkins,
     flatware)   _____

     Glassware   _____

☐ Labor (setup/cleanup,
food service, babysitter, etc.)   _____

☐   _____

Total $ _____

Questions to Ask a Party Planner

☐ Qualifications
- How long have you been planning events?
- Are you a Certified Special Events Professional (CSEP)?
- Have you planned events like mine before?
- Are you affiliated with any of the local or national event-planning associations?

☐ Fees
- What are your fees?
- What forms of payment do you accept?
- Can I revise the level of service I am purchasing?
- Do you require that I sign a contract to retain services?

☐ Style
- How will you communicate with me throughout the planning process?
- Will you be available to answer general party questions? Via phone? Via email?

☐ Other
- Can you work within my party budget?
- Do you have an assistant/backup in case you are ill or unable to attend my event?
- Are there local vendors you have worked with before whom you can recommend to me?
- Have you planned events at the location I am considering?

Easy Ways to Pick a Party Theme

☐ Find a cute invitation.

☐ Use the season as inspiration.

☐ Build a theme around the gift you have purchased for the guest of honor.

☐ Find a great deal on party supplies and work around the style.

☐ Google! Just search for the guest of honor's favorite things + "party" on Google Images and see what you get (i.e., "pedicure party").

Questions to Ask a Location Representative

☐ Is your location available on _____?

☐ How many people can you comfortably accommodate?

☐ Do you offer any event packages?

☐ Do you provide an event coordinator?

☐ What are your fees?

☐ Do you require a deposit to book your location?

☐ What forms of payment do you accept?

☐ Am I allowed to bring my own food or drinks?

☐ Do you have a list of recommended/approved vendors?

☐ Do you allow alcohol to be served?

☐ Do you provide tables, chairs, and linens?

☐ Do you provide assistance to set up and clean up?

☐ Can I access your location before the event to set up?

☐ Do you have any restrictions on the use of your space (decorations, games, etc.)?

☐ Are there any other policies I need to be aware of?

Tips for Being a Great Hostess

☐ Address invitations appropriately, and send them out well in advance of the event to allow ample time for guests to reply and make arrangements to attend.

☐ Be conscious of who you are inviting. If you are throwing a stock-the-bar party, you may not want to invite your friends who do not drink.

☐ Arrange additional help before the party if you need an extra set of hands to set up, clean up, or watch the kids. When in doubt, see if the teenager down the street is interested in helping for a few extra bucks.

☐ Greet guests when they arrive. If you are unavoidably detained, ensure that someone is there to greet guests at the door.

☐ Offer guests something to eat or drink as soon as you have taken their coat and bag.

☐ Take the time to chat with each of your guests throughout the event, and introduce guests to those they have not met before.

☐ Thank your guests as they leave and make sure they have their coats and bags.

☐ Give your guest of honor a Clueless Chick post-party kit.

Tips for Being a Great Guest

☐ Reply promptly to all invitations in the manner requested.

   ▪ If you misplace your invitation and do not have the hostess's contact information, ask the guest of honor for her phone number. Do not reply to the guest of honor—she should not be doing any work.

☐ Only those listed on your invitation are invited to the event.

   ▪ If the invitation was addressed to "Mr. and Mrs. Joe Wright," only the husband and wife are invited. Do not make the host uncomfortable by asking if she meant to invite your kids.

   ▪ If the invitation was addressed to "The Wright Family," the whole family is welcome to attend.

   ▪ If the invitation was addressed to a child, assume that one parent should attend as a chaperone unless the child is old enough to be dropped off.

☐ If something unavoidable arises after you have replied, call the hostess immediately to explain the situation.

☐ If you cannot find a sitter, send your regrets and a gift or note, if appropriate.

☐ Take a small hostess gift such as flowers, a bottle of wine, a picture frame, or a serving piece as a token of your gratitude.

☐ If you loved the event, let the host know by writing her a short note or sending a quick email.

Tips for Being a Great Guest of Honor

☐ Offer to help your host, even if you know she will not take you up on your offer.

☐ Ask if the host would like you to arrive at a special time.

☐ Thank your hostess by writing her a nice personal note or buying a small thank-you gift.

☐ Greet all of your guests and thank them for coming.

☐ Mingle! Make sure you have a chance to speak to everyone and introduce friends from different social circles to one another.

☐ Promptly send thank-you notes for any gifts you received to thank your friends for their thoughtfulness.

Party Setup Tips for The Clueless Chick™

When you are planning your party setup strategy, do not forget the 4 S's of setup: staging area, stations, storage, and simplify:

☐ Staging Area

- Create a staging area in an out-of-the-way (and out-of-sight) place, such as the laundry room, garage, or a closet, where you can stash extra food, containers, empty platters, etc.

- Make sure the dishwasher is empty before the party starts, so you can quickly and easily fill it with dirty dishes.

☐ Stations

- Create self-contained stations for food, drinks, activities, etc. Creating these designated areas will promote a natural flow and mingling during the party and prevent guests from needing to wander around trying to find a napkin when they are fixing a plate of food.

- Designate an area for guests to place gifts when they arrive. It is best if this is the same spot where gifts will be opened, so they do not have to be moved in the middle of the party. If, however, you will not be opening gifts during the party or are not expecting to receive gifts, put any gifts guests bring in another room, so as not to make other guests uncomfortable.

- Place trash receptacles in an easily accessible area and clearly label recycling and compost containers.

☐ Storage

- On a rainy day, have a bucket for wet umbrellas and an effective way to dry wet/muddy shoes.

- Designate an easily accessible area for coats, purses, diaper bags, etc.

☐ Simplify

- Wrapping silverware in a napkin makes it easier for guests to grab while they are fixing a plate of food and will encourage them to take only one set of flatware.

- Arrange seating so that guests do not need to move any furniture.

- Place coasters on all wood surfaces so that guests do not have to hunt for them.

- If you are expecting any babies or small children, make room for a diaper-changing area and place a stool in the bathroom so that little ones can reach the sink.

- Plan how you will send leftovers home with guests, so you are not scrambling at the end of the party.

- Consider placing favors by the door, so guests do not forget to take one.

And finally, the most important part of any setup—take pictures! Make sure you snap a few shots of your amazing handiwork before guests arrive.

Party Cleanup Tips for The Clueless Chick™

Cleanup can be overwhelming, especially when you are tired from all of the prep work, setup, and hosting. By taking a little time to plan ahead, you can avoid a number of headaches and ensure that your cleanup goes quickly and as smoothly as possible. When you are planning your party cleanup strategy, do not forget the 4 C's of cleanup; continuous, coordinated, careful, and consolidate:

☐ Continuous

- Clean as you go! If you can take a minute to pick up a dirty dish or put away an item no longer in use, you will save yourself time and make cleanup seem less daunting at the end of the party.
- Towards the end of the party, look through your storage area to ensure that no one has forgotten a coat, purse, etc.

☐ Coordinated

- Enlist help. Ask a friend or relative to chip in, or hire a local teen to help for an hour or so.
- Make sure you have a way to carry gifts out to the guest of honor's car.

☐ Careful

- Walk the entire party space twice to ensure you've gotten everything.
- Make sure the recycling is suitable to dump into the recycling bin. Ensure there isn't any recycling in your trash.

☐ Consolidate

- Move larger items to your staging area to get them out of the way.
- Quickly pack up leftovers by placing them back in their original packaging or prep/transport containers.